Dale Burk's
MONTANA

By Dale A. Burk

With a Foreword by Jack Weidenfeller

Enjoy —

Dale A. Burk

Dale Burk's

MONTANA

By Dale A. Burk

With a Foreword by Jack Weidenfeller

Copyright 2002 by Dale A. Burk

ISBN 1-931291-25-X (hardcover)
ISBN 1-931291-24-1 (softcover)

Library of Congress Card Number 2002094805

First Edition

Published in the United States of America

Text originally published in Montana, *by Dale A. Burk and Russell Lamb,© 1980, Graphic Arts Center Publishing®, an Imprint of Graphic Arts Center Publishing Company.*

STONEYDALE PRESS PUBLISHING COMPANY
523 Main Street • P.O. Box 188
Stevensville, Montana 59870
Phone: 406-777-2729

DEDICATION

Of the hundreds of individuals with whom I've shared the experience of witnessing the drama that is life in wild Montana, one person constantly comes to mind as the springboard from whence I launched my own intellectual inquiry into the processes that were shaping its and my destiny simultaneously. That person is Loren Kreck of Columbia Falls, Montana.

So clear, so profound, so undeniably poignant was his challenge to me, and others with us on an absolutely clear, stunning day in April of 1962, just under the Continental Divide on a spring excursion via ski and snowshoes to the Granite Park Chalet area in Glacier National Park, months before the park would be open to regular summer traffic, that it has both stuck with and motivated me to this day. I was just beginning to realize success then in my career as a writer-photographer, having returned to Montana to work as a journalist after a four-year stint overseas in the U.S. Navy. I was writing stories about Montana in various newspapers and national magazines at the time, but they were nice stories looking only at what we perceived as good things. Superficial I'd call them today. Why, Loren wondered, wasn't I asking questions, as a writer, about powerful forces, primarily out-of-state economic forces, that had launched, or were in the process of launching, enterprises that would literally change the face of Montana forever?

My recollection is that, on that particular day, I brushed his question off with the response that I wasn't in any position to make the sort of inquiry he suggested was needed. I had no "podium" from which to pursue the serious sort of work he was suggesting, and foresaw no real opportunity at the time to achieve one. But, as time went on, I realized that Loren Kreck had opened my eyes to look for things in the world around me that had previously been blocked out, truly ignored in my process of "seeing my world." He had changed me, and my life, forever. I began to "see" things that I'd never paid any attention to before. And he was right. Before my very eyes, water was being polluted, the air befouled, the forests literally overcut and multiple-use values violated to the point of devastation, wild free-flowing rivers were being silenced by one dam after another and dozens more were on the planning boards, the wild land that literally bespoke the quality that made Montana was being diminished day-by-day – and precious few questions were asked publicly about any of these things. I subsequently developed an attitude as a writer-journalist that while I might not know the answers to many of these impending issues, which came to be known as environmental problems everywhere in the country let alone Montana, I could always ask the questions about them that needed answering. Loren Kreck was right. I could help make the public aware of these things, so we could deal with them as a people. So began a change in my own life that has continued unabated to this day.

Little did I know then that my subsequent work as a writer for *The Missoulian*, the daily newspaper in Missoula, Montana, would lead to a number of national writing awards including becoming the first journalist working out of Montana to receive the prized Nieman Fellowship for Professional Journalists to Harvard University. That I would continue that work nationally over the next three decades. Or that I would work in concert with a friend named Loren Kreck as the chief instigators in achieving wilderness designation for a part of Montana now known as the Great Bear Wilderness, a legacy we share and cherish. The Great Bear, as well as many other things I've been involved in these past three decades, stem from that conversation Loren Kreck and I had so long, long ago on that high slope just under the Continental Divide. For that, for the earlier contribution he made to our nation and our way of life as a Marine fighter pilot in the Pacific in World War II, and his friendship and encouragement these many years, I thank him – and make the dedication of this book to him. He is a true Montana hero.

TABLE OF CONTENTS

Cover Photo: Reflection of Stanton Lake and Stanton Glacier in the Great Bear Wilderness in northwestern Montana. This and all other photos in this book were taken by the author. His first hike into this stunning section of terrain that would ultimately become the Great Bear Wilderness was at the age of thirteen on a trip with his paternal grandmother.

Preceding pages:
The lightning photograph was taken by the author on an overnight excursion to the Granite Park Chalet area in Glacier National Park. It is one of a series he captured of a thunder and lightning storm that moved northward, over a two-hour period in the middle of the night, from Heaven's Peak to the Livingston Range, the setting of this photograph with multiple lightning strikes, and then eastward to the Continental Divide.

ACKNOWLEDGMENTS

The making of a book is an effort requiring the participation of many people. This one is no exception. Over the years, countless friends, associates and family members assisted in the making of many of the photographs that appear in this book — particularly in regard to their patience while waiting for me to "get" the picture I wanted. Sometimes, by the way, that waiting stretched into hours as I held out for the just-right light or some other element of emphasis. The final selection, from several thousand photographs, of those that appear in this book was accomplished with the assistance of four people in particular, my wife, Patricia, and Rachel Courteau, Jeanne O'Neill and Riga Winthrop, photographers all and the latter two being members of the famed Discovery Writers of Stevensville, Montana. Bob Hafer of Victor, Montana, a computer genius, was most helpful in terms of production questions, and so was the professional advice provided by Dwight Tompkins and Jeri Reese of Walsworth Publishing Company. I am also grateful for the ongoing encouragement, over many years, from three people in particular to put this sort of book together: artists Elmer Sprunger of Bigfork and Bob Morgan of Helena, plus Jack Weidenfeller of Missoula, who generously provided a Foreword for this book.

FOREWORD

Dale Burk is in love with Montana. This book is his tribute to the state that is the love of his life, a place, a land, a spirit that in its non-uniformity and majestic grandeur not only inspires awe and captures imagination, but evokes a loyalty and in turn a responsibility to recognize its beauty and conserve its riches. In this book, Dale, whose third-generation roots lie deep in northwestern Montana, succeeds in painting a picture of Montana's geological and cultural diversity, of its history and the impact of the people who have shaped it and scarred it, and of the current struggle to control the forces both within and without the state that are continually besieging this "one of a kind" place; forces that lust for its riches and for a way of life that is in danger of being smothered into a cultural sameness that can only be defined as "Americanized."

Within the pages of this book, both in text and photographs, the reader will discover the unbelievable vastness of Montana, dotted by busy pulsating cities, small town communities, ghost towns, farms, ranches, forest, lakes and streams, wild lands and wild creatures, parks, both Glacier and Yellowstone, public lands, mighty rivers, towering cliff-faced mountains, badlands, and prairies with acres of grassland wrapped by fences. Here history makers such as Lewis and Clark open up the land of treasure to the fur traders and gold miners, missionaries arrive to bring Christianity to the Indians, great corporations such as the Anaconda Copper Mining Company strangle the political life of the state during is tenure, lumberjacks toil in the western forests, writers and artists capture the moments that define Montana's heritage. Hours of research have been compacted into statistics that are sometimes inscrutable and sometimes overwhelming, such as Montana encompasses over 147,000 square miles; two million acres of Montana's land are utilized in irrigated farming, roughly twelve million acres in dry-land farming and the remaining forty-eight million in livestock grazing. Montana boasts 450 miles of "blue-ribbon" trout streams. The state is 547 miles wide from east to west and underneath its eastern agricultural lands lie, perhaps, 350 billion tons of coal.

Dale has taken all the photographs displayed in this book. Over the years, he has worked as a journalist, author, photographer, teacher, publisher, conservationist and political activist. Dale does not hesitate to step into the controversy over preserving versus exploitation of Montana's wild lands and wildlife. He has worked for years to establish and protect wilderness areas in Montana, helped spearhead the campaign to designate the Great Bear Wilderness and the establishment of wild rivers and wildlife refuges, protect key wildlife habitat, and has been honored with many national awards from the likes of Trout Unlimited, the American Motors National Conservation Award, the Sierra Club, and in 1975 was the first journalist working out of Montana to receive a prestigious Nieman Fellowship for Professional Journalists to Harvard University. His most prized forms of recognition, however, are two-fold: receiving a Lifetime Membership Award from the Montana Wilderness Association and being named to the Montana Hunting Hall of Fame because of his writing on wildlife and conservation issues.

In this book, *"Dale Burk's Montana,"* he clarifies the context in which we face contention today over this place called Montana and asks questions vital to the future of the state. For readers who know and love Montana, these original pictures will illuminate regions seldom seen, stir up memories, inform and evoke sentiments of pride and attachment, of anxiety and defensiveness. Readers unfamiliar with Montana will find in the pages of this book romance, unforgettable scenes of fierce and majestic beauty, pock-marked history and haunting questions in the context of the writer's passion for a land that has been described as "uncommon" and "nothing better anywhere else."

Jack Weidenfeller
Missoula, Montana
September 26, 2002

INTRODUCTION

I am one of those blessed creatures who knew as a youngster that a certain place had a special hold on me and that, given the ability to control my destiny, it would be where I'd live out my life. That place is known as Montana.

The realization of this truth came at an early age, consciously in my teens when I left the state to serve three years overseas in the U.S. Navy but more likely subconsciously long before that. After all, it was growing up in a logging family on the very fringes of both wild and settled Montana in northwestern Montana that I bonded with this incredible "place." That was more than six decades ago.

At the time I had no way of knowing that this bond would become a mindset, nor that I would develop an unshakable conviction that those of us who live and work in this incredible land have been given both opportunity and responsibility to realize its bounty and to care for this thing we call place. Change was, of course, occurring even when I was a youngster, but change then, in the 1940s and early 1950s, was neither obvious nor exponential to any but the trained eye. But it was occurring. Perhaps it was a product of my own naivete, but if so it was a naivete shared by the majority of those of us who lived here then. What we were doing, had done, would do, was in the very process of changing Montana forever and, by and large, we didn't even know it. Or realize then that not all those changes were good. We just accepted things as they were and expected the way of life we enjoyed would last forever.

Recent years, however, altered both that mindset and our actions, individually and as a community. There was a time when Montana was relatively unknown to most Americans. After all, it was truly the outback place, the Siberia of America, among the last places most people would think of as a land to move to, to settle. Montana was out beyond the realm of reality for most Americans, not all but most. Time, of course, changed that perception, too, coupled with technological advances of transportation and communication.

It became possible, indeed a reality, to both live in Montana and work in the mainstream of American economic and political life. Such changes meant, of course, that the Montana of my youth was gone forever.

With those changes came increased visibility to all America of both the incredible variation in natural wonders we lived among in Montana, and took for granted, and the opportunity to live and work in their midst. Without realizing it, those of us who had been here before the big change began had to adjust our physical and emotional, even spiritual, mindsets to changes that were, literally, beyond our individual control. Changes that march onward, for good or bad, even today.

So what does all this mean to those of us who identify with Montana today, visitor and resident alike? It is a special place. And even with the overwhelming changes of recent years, I still want and choose to live here. It may be a place shared with growing numbers of people, but it is still mine, "my Montana". Individually, personally, mine in a non-possessive sense knowing that while I make that claim I can do so only in the reality that I am but a visitor identifying with this place for the very, very short time in relationship to its ongoing geologic history and my comparatively brief individual lifetime.

The essay you read in this book appears in slightly revised form from its original appearance a number of years ago in another book titled "Montana" that I co-authored. It is, however, mostly unchanged from what I wrote originally at the request of a man named Charles H. Belding, whose publishing company, Graphic Arts Publishing of Portland, Oregon, issued large-format photo-text essay books on elements of American geography. A marvelous personality and exceptionally-gifted photographer named Russell Lamb and I collaborated on that book to excellent reviews at the time. But like many such publications, it went through several editions and ultimately was taken out of print. In recent years I've had many requests for copies of that book, so it was natural to pursue the notion of a new publication of my original text in book form, along with a number of my own photographs. Thus, the concept presented in this format was born – a special presentation of "Dale Burk's Montana." As a writer, photographer, commentator, citizen-activist, and third-generation resident of Montana, I've both witnessed and participated in the process of change in Montana over a lifetime that began as the child of a logging family in northwestern Montana and continues as a writer-publisher based in the Bitterroot Valley of southwestern Montana. I still marvel, each day as I awaken to the play of a new and never-the-same sunrise sculpting the lofty Bitterroot Range to the west of my home in Stevensville, that Montana is a marvelous, magical place. It is a place that holds me firmly in its grip just as it did when it first locked itself in my heart when I was a boy. I hope that, in the essay that follows, some of the almost unbelievable magic of this place — "my Montana" — unfolds for you to enjoy, and ponder, too.....

Dale A. Burk
Stevensville, Montana
August 22, 2002

Sunrise spreads a glow of expectancy across eastern Montana.

MONTANA

One's perception of Montana, today, stems not so much from what it is as what one brings to it. It is a land, at once, of jagged mountains, snowy peaks, high prairie, badlands, wild river and wheat wrested from a moisture-slaked earth, of forests and grass-lands, sometimes intermingled, and, always, awesome panorama and tremendous distance. But what it is can depend on how you choose to see those things.

Montana has been described as a state of mind. It is that, and more. Native and newcomer alike must come to grips, in a very personal sense, with a schizophrenic piece of geography that spans the high plains and the northern Rockies. Montana is not a place like anywhere else. It is itself, inviting and still foreboding, delicately gentle in proper season and yet, at times, uncompromisingly brutal. It is a large, diverse, fertile land that demands you accept it on its terms – whatever you want of it.

Those terms are written on the face of its land. They are, ultimately, its uniqueness, its eloquent, pervasive soul. They bespeak, in the unpredictability of wind and rain and breezeless sun, in the uncertainty of season, of a God who made a land where the forces of nature rule. So it is in Montana, be it mountain or prairie. This is an exquisite area where you never escape closeness with it and the forces that shape it. It gives you no option, and never has.

Still, there are – as there always have been – many Montanas. We look at the land, the same land, differently; one man's wild river is another's power impoundment, one conglomerate's strip mine is home to a community of ranchers, and so on, ad infinitum. One shapes one's own perception to suit one's whims or needs. Or ambitions. Always, in reality as in perceiving, there is contention. Montana is, and always has been, the home of competition for it. It is a rich prize, this magnificent land, worth defending. Or contending for. The proud Blackfeet Indians thought so, for sure, in their time. So did the resourceful fur trader and then the miner and, subsequently, the lumberjack, the hunter, the cattleman, and the sodbuster and merchant.

But times change. Now, as earlier, the contention is for the region and what it offers. For the Blackfeet it was home and hearth, a way of life, civilization as they knew it. For the miner it was gold and silver and, later, enormous amounts of copper. And undreampt of wealth. Now it's coal, billions of pounds of it, water and gas and oil and timber, and things taken for granted earlier, things like wild, free-flowing rivers, wilderness and wildlife that no longer is plentiful.

What is this place Montana? How did it come to be and what shape shall its destiny take? And what of its people? Its natural life community? Its natives, people and wildlife alike, were rudely, relentlessly shoved aside, ignored, overwhelmed, subjugated. Is the same fate in store for those who now call its environs home – whatever their perception?

Now, as before, the answer eludes us. We can speak only in maybes and ifs and hopes and dreams, for the forces that shape that destiny come from beyond that place we call Montana. Its magnificence, its richness of coal, water and oil, and wilderness and wild river have made it the battleground, and the prize, of numerous vying forces. And the war is going on right now, its outcome still in doubt, its results still unknown. Be it enough, for now, that we know that this land is still the center of contention.

Even so, it still is a land where poetry can be found flowing in the morning wind. With all its change, Montana is a place of beauty and timelessness. It holds now, as it did in 1841 when the Jesuit, Father Nicolas Point, penned the following words, a romance that captures one's imagination and sharpens judgment and one's sense of being in the right place: "On September 24, (1841) we emerged from the gorge called Hell Gate onto a broad plain, bordered on the north by the country of the Pend d'Oreilles and on the west by that of the Coeur d' Alenes. But finding nothing there to suit our purpose, we turned south through a gorge, at first narrow, but then ever widening. A day later, the third day of our search, we had still found nothing by evening. But arriving at the foot of the largest mountain in the vicinity, we were agreeably surprised at the richness of the vegetation stretched out before us. This luxuriance was due to two streams running north. This large valley, protected against the Blackfeet on the south by a chain of mountains on whose slopes grew forests, so necessary as a source of construction materials. Between these two ranges ran the river of the Flatheads, called

Preceding page:
Daylight penetrates the famed Danaher Basin in the Bob Marshall
Wilderness.

the Bitter Root River. Everyone thought we would be able to find nothing better anywhere else." – *Wilderness Kingdom,* The Journals of Nicolas Point, S.J.: Holt, Rinehart and Winston, Publishers, 1967.

Most Montanans today would agree with that, be they situated in the Bitterroot Valley only a mile or so from my home, as Father Point was when he wrote those words, or on the rich grasslands adjoining the Missouri Breaks. Montana is that just-right place; search as you might, "...we would be able to find nothing better anywhere else."

This attitude is not without its detractors. Not long ago an out-of-state land developer friend, himself a former Montanan, bemoaned Montanans' prideful possessiveness of their native land. He called it conceit worse than he'd found among Texans for their state. He was reacting, of course, to the protective legislation. Montanans had passed to preserve some portions of the state, and while his observation was self-serving it also was accurate. People tend to *care* about the place in which they

A lone boatman pursues a dream on gigantic Flathead Lake in northwestern Montana.

live.

Most of them, too, possess a general understanding of the historical events that have shaped them – at least insofar as the Lewis and Clark Expedition, the fur trappers, gold miners and copper barons are concerned. Millions of words have been written of those eras; they are the romance and legend upon which we base the notion of our culture, our tie to the past. Less is known of the period before them, or since, though those periods also shape the imagination, the perception, of our land and who and what we are as a people, we Montanans.

It is enough, for now, for us to accept things as they are. Those geological forces, the upheavals, twistings and turnings, the grinding and crushing of glaciers, plus countless centuries of unrelenting winds and rain and cold have given us a diverse land both fertile and, in places, barren. It is sufficient that we have learned, are learning, to live with it, to understand it, to accept it, to extol its virtues and shortcomings alike in their naturalness.

How does one get a grasp of this place Montana? It is so huge, 147,134 square miles, so diverse in terrain and environment, so unlike, from one region to another, in occupation and potential, that it defies singular definition. Or understanding. Montana is a complex place, whatever perception you use to understand it. Be it geography, natural history, or human enterprise – you're likely to find incredible, perhaps unbelievable, differences in the land, its flora and fauna, and its people within a few miles almost anywhere in the state.

The Federal Writer's Project described it thusly in its Depression-initiated book about the state published in 1939:

"Montana is too large and diverse for definition or characterization in general terms. Children in its schools are taught that the name Montana means "mountains," but many of them see only prairies rolling to the horizon. They are told that Montana is still a great ranching state, where cattle graze and cowboys ride, but some of them, as in Butte, see only ore dumps, great dark sheds, and barren buttes.

"To the dry-land farmer in the eastern part of the state, Montana is a vast agricultural plain checkered with brownish fallow land and fields of green wheat that ripen to a dusty gray-gold in August; or it is a drab waste seen through a haze of wind-blown soil. For him the mountains of the western part exist chiefly as the goal for some long-deferred vacation.

"To the resident of the mountain region, Montana is a land of rich valleys, small thriving cities, and uncounted mineral treasures. He hesitates to admit that anything important or interesting can exist in the immensities of dead brown grass and gray stubble that make up the eastern two-thirds of his state. At best, he believes, tank towns are there, and cattle and wheat. Less than best means badlands, coyotes, tumbleweeds, and dust."

Generally, the state is divided into two regions: the mountainous one-third at the western end and the high plains and undulating prairie of the eastern two-thirds. That is a division that is cultural as well as geographical. Here, if nowhere else in the country, it can be shown that the land and its values shape the people and theirs. Agriculture has been dominant in the eastern part of the state, though it now is contending to preserve its values against the strip miners. Logging, mining and, nowadays, wilderness preservation, are major forces in the starkly beautiful mountains to the west.

The Continental Divide, throughout its serpentine length, in Montana, is a natural and metaphorical barrier between these regions. It always has been; even prehistoric peoples perceived it as a religious as well as physical separation of one part of the land from another.

Preceding pages:
Below zero in southwestern Montana.   *A field of ripening wheat aglow under the rays of an evening sun.*

One place along that divide, I think, gives special insight to its life-shaping influence on the northern Rocky Mountain region. It is in Glacier National Park and I went there one cold, snow-swept day recently to glimpse once again this timeless sentinel of a land's origin. It is Triple Divide Peak.

Now Triple Divide isn't the most awesome mountain in Glacier Park; indeed, it is quite plain in comparison to its kin in Glacier. But unlike the others, it generates on its sedimentary slopes the water to feed three distant oceans – the Pacific, Gulf of Mexico and Hudson Bay. It is a starting point for three of the world's greatest watersheds, the place at which nature's most important life-giving force, water, begins its pulsating journey to the ocean. In the process, it helps shape the destiny of mighty regions in the drainage basins of the Columbia, the Missouri and the Saskatchewan and Nelson Rivers in Canada.

From Triple Divide, and other mountains in Glacier, Montana spreads before like an unending panorama in any direction you look. To the east are the high plains, closely serrated by deep-cut canyons and vast ridges whose north slopes are dusk-green with pine and fir; beyond the tawny grass takes over and the ridges flatten. In the distance, the land seems flat, gentle, though you know it is not. To the north and south and west, the eye beholds only mountains. Vast, unending mosaics of cliffs and clefts, of valleys and rushing rivers and peaks brushed with snow among the verdant slopes and, here and there, remnant glaciers. It appears an impenetrable, impassable land, this topsy-turvy thrust of peak upon mountain peak, but again you know better. The land is more than it seems.

Montana is captive to its geologic past. The same forces that wrought its beauty gave it its wealth. To the early prospectors and the miners who followed them, gold, silver and copper made it the "Treasure State." To many people of kindred spirit it is so even today, though the gold diggings have worn out and the others had trod much the same path. They exist, but they're dying; mineral wealth, ultimately, is exhaustible. Only coal, once ignored but now invaluable to a world glutinous over energy, holds hope for big diggings – though an open-pit copper mine at Butte remains a stark reminder of more lusty days on this place the miners called "The Richest Hill on Earth."

Others have seen wealth in the natural beauty; it is wealth of the spirit, of recreation of one's inner being, of harmony with the world about them. And this is not

Stunning panorama of the Garden Wall in Glacier National Park hovering over McDonald Creek on the west side of the park.

just a recent fad, or an outgrowth of the environmental awareness of the 1970s. Montana's first recorded visitors, the Lewis and Clark Expedition led by Captains Meriwether Lewis and William Clark, made note of these qualities during their epic journey.

Consider, for example, this excerpt from Lewis' journal, written in 1805 as the Lewis and Clark Expedition trudged its way up the Missouri River in what now is north-central Montana:

"As usual, saw great quantity of game today: buffalo, elk, goats or antelopes feeding in every direction. We kill whatever we wish ... the country is as yesterday beautiful in the extreme."

It has been that way since. A portion of Yellowstone National Park is in Montana; what is generally unknown about this park, the first and philosophic mainspring of the national park idea, is that several of Montana's pioneer citizens took an active part in

The junction of the Missouri and Marias Rivers, a point the Lewis and Clark Expedition labeled "Camp Decision," looking downstream. They properly judged the left fork (at the right in this photo) to be the Missouri.

meetings where the notion of establishing a natural, national park was brought to fruition.

Montana's people, from the beginning, have been as contradictory, as complex as the land itself. One part booster-developer and another preservationist, they, too must appear schizophrenic to those trying to understand them.

For practical purposes, Montana's modern-day history begins with the Lewis and Clark Expedition. It was they, more than any others, who triggered the subsequent influx of trappers and fur traders into the region.

Lewis and Clark spent more time, and traveled more miles, in Montana than any other to-be-state on their epic journey. And glowing reports were made of its untold wealth in beaver and other furs, of its rich lands, forested slopes and severe, unpredictable climate. Evidence of their journey abounds today.

Roadside signs provide constant reminders: Lewis and Clark Trail. So do special

Thousands of beaver impoundments on the mountain streams at the headwaters of the Missouri would, in the wake of the Lewis and Clark Expedition, entice hordes of trappers (mountain men) into the region.

remnants, like Pompey's Pillar along the Yellowstone east of Billings. Here, on July 25, 1806, Captain William Clark named what he called a remarkable rock in honor of Sacajawea's young son. It is the only remaining visible legacy of the expedition on the state landscape, his name and the date carved in the soft limestone. That rock now is a national monument.

All of the many Lewis and Clark routes that traversed our state on *their* eastward and westward journeys are well marked. So are many of their campsites, where known or discerned from their journals. One of the most renowned is at the mouth of Lolo Creek in the Bitterroot Valley; called Traveler's Rest, they rested here twice, once in September of 1805 before crossing over "these tremendous mountains" into the Lochsa River country to make their run to the Pacific Ocean and again in early July of 1806 on their return journey. This site is now a Montana State Park.

Nothing Lewis and Clark said, however, could have enticed "civilization" to Montana so quickly as did the finding of gold on Grasshopper Creek near the present town of Bannack in 1862. To be sure, this wasn't the first find of this precious metal in Montana. That had occurred ten years earlier when Francis Finlay made his initial discovery at Gold Creek, a tributary of the Clark Fork between what is now Drummond and Garrison, southeast of Missoula and northwest of Deer Lodge.

The Grasshopper diggings were big, however, and soon word of the find got out! The result was an influx of prospectors and miners and highwaymen that would change, for all time, the land to become known as Montana. Gold was to be found. Gold! Riches for the taking and a chance at inconsumable wealth – or, at the hands of a highly-organized band of outlaws, death.

Other finds followed. The Grasshopper diggings yielded millions in gold. Rich Alder Gulch and its center, Virginia City, followed and it was much richer. So did Confederate Gulch, Last Chance Gulch (modern-day Helena) and Marysville, and lesser diggings. Montana became a territory and, ultimately, a state.

Meanwhile, the gold began to play out and for a time it appeared that Montana's diggings would experience the same fate as others elsewhere. Indeed, most of the Montana strikes became, in the tradition of the gold fields, ghost towns.

Such was not to be the case with a high headwaters valley tucked just west of a jag in the Continental Divide in southwestern Montana. Its gold played out, too, but a silver boom kept the thriving area of Butte alive as a mining camp. And then, in 1876,

Southwestern Montana

a shrewd young Irish orphan-immigrant who stands even today as an example of the Horatio Alger "rags to riches" story, realized the real wealth that lay beneath Butte Hill. Copper, Marcus Daly said, was to be the metal of the future – and his insight made him a multimillionaire and the first and most powerful of Montana's copper kings. Some historians credit his great rival, William Andrews Clark, with perceiving the riches to be made in copper. However the fact remains that it was Daly's technical skill and contacts with outside wealth that provided the keys to opening up Butte's rich copper depositions.

It was a mine Daly shrewdly and quietly bought into that bore the name of his empire, Anaconda. It became an appendage equally loathed and feared across decades of Montana history from the time Daly built his empire around it.

Other empires have been built in Montana, too. None have come close to matching the A-C-M – it most always has been known by its initials, representing Anaconda Copper Mining Company, whatever subtle name changes the enterprise used – in terms of economic and political power. For at least two generations it treated Montana as the economic fiefdom it was. That began to change in the mid-1960s and today The Anaconda Company no longer exists, and its successor, Atlantic Richfield, is a potent force but it has to share its economic and political clout with others.

Politics change and so does the land. The Montana of Lewis and Clark and the fur trappers and the early settlers exists largely in our memories and legends. Time would have had it otherwise, as those few remnants of untouched wilderness tell us. But this land Montana could not remain a wilderness, once the white man came with his ways

of life. The era of the nomadic, hunter-savage ended with the first glitter of gold in the Grasshopper diggings as surely as if, *ex cathedra,* a proclamation declaring its to-be-demise had been issued. It simply took another forty years for it to achieve its inevitable fate. Progress, the march of civilization, Manifest Destiny – or whatever other euphemism was used – throbbed unabated over the land. First it was the miner and then, in his support, the timberman and the cattleman. Next it was the sheepman and then came the sodbuster-homesteader, fences, and, ultimately, the big farmers and dams that stilled the once-rushing rivers and fed irrigation water to previously-dry fields. Somewhere in there, too, oil was discovered and pipelines began to join the growing network of railroads and highways and electrical transmission lines. Each, indelibly, scratched its mark on the Montana landscape and the consciousness of its people. Somehow, we assured ourselves, things were better and yet as the 1970s told us, that was not necessarily the case.

The change, it seemed, needed monitoring. Direction. A new ethical base. Once-clean streams lay polluted, running red with the filth of raw waste and, in places, the air was harsh and unfit to breathe as industrial pollutants spewed into the atmosphere. Subdivision development invaded, uncontrolled, critical wildlife habitat areas and gobbled up thousands of acres of prime farmland.

Miles of internationally-renowned trout streams suffered channelization by heavy equipment or, at the minimum, streambed disruption that destroyed aquatic insect life and fish habitat. The result was a decline in the quality of human life as well as the state's once-great fishing streams.

On the fir and pine-covered slopes of western Montana, outcries against a timber-cutting practice known as clearcutting, led from our famed Bitterroot National Forest, to national hearings and ultimate passage of two pieces of reform legislation affecting the entire national forest system. Simultaneously, an emotive campaign led by citizen-conservationists sought protection for some of Montana's ever-diminishing wilderness resource, an issue that is always present at the forefront of Montana political life.

Residents reacted to these problems in typical fashion. Vigilante-like, they set out to do something about it themselves. In a few short years from 1969 through 1974, they passed a dozen or more pieces of environmental legislation that stand as exemplary challenges to the nation. Thus they serve not so much to prevent development but to direct and control it so it is not destructive of the qualities that prevail in the region.

Preceding page:
The Beartooth plateau.

Timbering practices that emphasized clearcutting and overcutting of timber, plus excessive roading in balance with other multiple-use values like watershed protection, wildlife, recreation and esthetics on the Bitterroot National Forest in Montana, and elsewhere on the national forest system, led to reform forestry legislation aimed at correcting such abuses. These scenes are on the Bitterroot National Forest.

For example, those "reformation" years also saw the state write a new constitution – and two of its most significant provisions were aimed at preserving aspects of Montana life considered sacrosanct. Those include one for direct citizen involvement in government – the initiative. The other was a constitutional guarantee of a clean and healthful environment. Combined with other inalienable rights, Montanans thus guaranteed themselves conditions amenable to protecting and preserving the quality of life in their state-and the method of guaranteeing that quality. The message of the 1972 constitution was clear and in recent years the very wordage of that constitution, as well as the philosophy behind it, has been upheld in the face of court actions trying to weaken it.

No longer would the people tolerate activities that deplete or destroy those very things that make it unique. Montana, the "last of the big time splendors" as state travel officials touted it, wanted to stay that way.

So where does that leave us. Montana is a land of magnificent wilderness and big, open vistas we call "Big Sky Country". It was extracted from the phrase, and book title, coined by Montana's most honored literary figure, novelist A. B. "Bud" Guthrie, Jr. But it also is a land of family farm and corporate agribusiness, of oil wells, wheat fields, logger and lumberman, of miner in quest yet of gold and copper, coal and newer metals like molybdenum, of Indian reservations, manufacturing and cottage industry; furthermore towns to serve them all, colleges, clubs and clusters of communities locked in the grip of by-gone days.

Montana is, in many ways, a lot like anyplace else in spite of what its people might like to believe about it or themselves. And why not! It is part of the greater, bland cultural milieu now shaping a gray sameness to our cities and towns everywhere in the country. The vista on many Montana streets, indeed even in many of its smaller towns, is no different than in, say, Boise, Idaho, or Skokie, Illinois, or Memphis, Tennessee.

Traffic lights, street intersections, hamburger stands and bank buildings, they all tend to look alike, wherever they are. Indeed, they often are alike, or identical. There's no escaping the great leveling force of conformity and universality. To some degree or another, most Montana communities, as we crawl into the early years of a new century, march in lock-step with the pulse-beat that shapes life in other American communities.

Still, one fact remains irrefutable. Those conformities, those similarities to Skokie

Preceding page:
Sunset on Flathead Lake.

The Stillwater River in northwestern Montana

Contrasting evenings in Montana. Below, in the upper Blackfoot River. Above, a deep draw in eastern Montana.

and what-have-you exist only in man-made things. Natural Montana, geographic Montana remains unique, apart, aloof even with its changes. Some would say majestic. It seems, to some degree, timeless and unchanging whatever man has wrought within it. The harsh snows come with the regularity of the season, the rivers flow and in forest and grassland alike the ageless wind ripples across the brow of the land to remind us of the ages past and yet to come.

We are here but for a time, but ah, what a land in which to be. Surely Lewis and Clark had no richer, fuller chance than we. There is less of some things, sure, but more of others – like appreciation. We *know* the value of things in short supply; we realize, unlike them, the privilege of being settlers rather than sojourners. This land, as it is, is ours. It is home; we are possessors and are richer for that relationship.

Let us, then, take a look at this Montana of today and in the process, reminisce a little. We'll understand it better if we do. Some of the events of the past couple hundred years give special meaning to the land we cherish.

One constant is its setting. Canada is to the north. Montana shares 550 miles of international boundary along the 49th parallel with, from the west, British Columbia, Alberta and Saskatchewan. This is all mountainous country west of the Continental Divide; to the east in Alberta the mountains quickly give way to the high plains and the prairie.

The border with Idaho zigs and zags along the top of stark mountain ridges; they form a ragged southeasterly arc and then an eastward plunge to Wyoming – which shares with Idaho the southern extent of Montana. Idaho's boundary is basically geographic. For the most part it follows sharp mountain ridges and, at Montana's southern extreme, the Continental Divide. Such is not the case with Wyoming.

Here it is a latitudinal line – the 45th parallel – that separates the Treasure and Cowboy States; never mind that they share a portion of Yellowstone Park and remarkably similar terrain at the eastern extreme of each state. Maybe it simply took someone drawing a line on a map to differentiate between them here.

Much the same could be said of Montana's eastern end on the 104th meridian. The Dakotas, North and South, bound it here – prairie land, grass and badlands. The same? Not hardly, no matter if it *looks* alike. Montana's different, in imagination and hope, if nothing else. Why this is the land where Custer and his men suffered complete annihilation, where the early fur trappers along the Yellowstone River and the upper Missouri centered. It was here, to the west of that meridian, that history counted. In

Montana! And even if you can't see the difference, assuming you are a Montanan, you can feel it.

Pundits like to alliterate on the "from Eureka to Ekalaka" bit to emphasize the breadth of Montana, and right they are. It is a long ways across the state, but I like to refer to it as being as long as the alphabet – from the tiny hamlet of Alzada in the southeastern-most corner of the state to Yaak, with its famous Dirty Shame Saloon, as its most northwesterly community.

Whatever, it takes some traveling to get across Montana. The state is 550 miles wide – east to west, that is – and 275 to 325 miles north-to-south. You could lose all of New England *in* it, plus a good share of the other Atlantic seaboard states. The same yardstick applies should you compare it with Japan, which is roughly the same size as Montana.

Distances deceive, however, in places like Montana. You generally find it impossible to travel in a straight line in mountainous country; consequently, you actually

Evening rainbow.

travel more miles eastward from Missoula to Sidney, Montana, than from Missoula to Seattle, Washington, or Portland, Oregon, and 100 of those miles westward would still be in Montana!

Much of Montana's vast landscape is, fortunately, still in public ownership. Access and use are consequently subject to the long-term public interest.

Some 37 percent of Montana is under federal administration. This includes 16.7 million acres under jurisdiction of the U.S. Forest Service, most of it in Montana's timbered mountainous country. There are, however, some national grasslands involved on the Custer National Forest in southeastern Montana.

The Bureau of Land Management is responsible for 7.2 million acres of public domain land, most of it in the form of intermingled ownership with private lands east of the Continental Divide. Much of the public domain land represents productively-low agricultural land no one wanted during homesteading days; today its value as grazing land is unequaled in many areas.

Other major federal landowners include the National Park Service, 1.1 million

acres, the Army Corps of Engineers, U.S. Fish and Wildlife Service, Bureau of Reclamation, Veterans Administration and the Bureau of Indian Affairs. Lesser amounts are controlled by the U.S. Air Force, Army, Agricultural Research Service, and the Veterans Administration.

In addition, some 6 million acres – most of it a result of school grants – is owned by the State of Montana.

Eleven federal wilderness areas have been established on the national forests in Montana and eleven others involving an additional million acres are under study for possible inclusion in the National Wilderness Preservation System.

Those already classified include the Bob Marshall Wilderness on the Flathead and Lewis and Clark National Forests, 1,009,356 acres; Absaroka-Beartooth on the Custer and Gallatin National Forests, 921,583 acres; Anaconda-Pintler on the Beaverhead, Bitterroot and Deer Lodge National Forests, 158,526 acres; Cabinet Mountains on the Kootenai Forest, 94,272 acres; Gates of the Mountains on the Helena National Forest, 28,562 acres; Great Bear on the Flathead National Forest, 286,700 acres; Mission Mountains on the Flathead National Forest, 73,877; Lincoln-Scapegoat on the Helena, Lewis and Clark and Lolo National Forests, 239,936 acres; Welcome Creek on the Lolo National Forest, 28,135 acres; and the Selway-Bitterroot (Montana portion) on the Bitterroot and Lolo National Forests, 406,450 acres. The Selway-Bitterroot straddles the Bitterroot Mountains in Montana and Idaho, for a grand total of 1,235,081 acres.

In addition the national forest land provides the watershed for one of Montana's two components of the National Wild and Scenic Rivers System – 219 miles of the North, South and Middle Forks of the Flathead River. The other wild river component is on the Missouri River in north-central Montana. Here the late U.S. Senator Lee Metcalf led a long effort to preserve 149 miles of the river, extending from Fort Benton to the Fred Robinson Bridge within the C. M. Russell Wildlife Refuge, as a wild, free-flowing stream. No dams will ever still the waters of this portion of the Missouri, or the three headwaters forks of the Flathead.

Few characteristics shape Montana's life qualities more than altitude. Butte and Helena, for example, are both high on opposite flanks of the Continental Divide – if some sixty-plus miles apart. They're well above a mile-high in elevation, but still pikers compared to that Montana community familiar to weather-watchers nationwide: West Yellowstone.

Selway-Bitterroot Wilderness.

West Yellowstone, at 6,665 feet elevation on the western edge of Yellowstone National Park, often makes the daily weather tally on national television for being the coldest place in the nation. Small wonder, that high up the mountain. But then, another familiar name on that tally sheet is Cut Bank, Montana, exposed as it is on the high prairie just east of the Rocky Mountains and just inside Montana where arctic blasts from Canada often lock it in icy grips for weeks at a time.

Neither, however, has the distinction of being the coldest place in Montana. That belongs to a spot northwest of Helena and east of Lincoln, just west of the Continental Divide. Here, one cold January night in 1954, the temperature hit minus 70 degrees Fahrenheit, the coldest ever recorded in the forty-eight contiguous United States. Brrrr. Before that, the state's coldest spot had existed at Fort Keough in Custer County, where it dove to minus 65 degrees Fahrenheit on January 15, 1888.

Most of the time, even in winter, it is not anywhere near that bad. Montana's mean annual temperature is 42.6. Its hottest was 117 and, in July and August, it often reaches 100. July is normally the warmest month, January the coldest.

Most of Montana's major valleys, like the historic Bitterroot and the Flathead, are near 3,400 feet in altitude. For comparison, scenic Bozeman Valley is closer to 4,500 feet above sea level.

Montana's highest point is Granite Peak, 12,799 feet, in the Beartooth Mountains of south central Montana. Its lowest is across the state near Troy where, at 1,885 feet, the Kootenai River leaves the northwest corner of the state to flow into Idaho. Then due east across the state, the altitude at Fairview where the Yellowstone River leaves Montana is 1,902 feet. That's close enough to merit mentioning both!

It also is interesting from the perspective of "leveling out" distance from the Continental Divide. The Kootenai River's exit from Montana is approximately 200 miles west of the Continental Divide; Montana here is precipitous mountainous country. It drops quickly. East of the divide it's a different story. Fairview is fully 350 miles east of the Continental Divide in central Montana, perhaps 250 from the jag the divide makes into Wyoming at the headwaters of the Yellowstone. It takes a lot longer to lose elevation in the prairie country.

One wonders, then, how best to "see" Montana. We can meander, for instance, from the headwaters of the Missouri into its famous Three Forks country and the main Big Muddy and its historic but aptly illustrative bromide: "too thick to drink and too

The Kootenai River in northwestern Montana.

thin to plow." Or we can float the rushing wild, free-flowing waters on the western slopes. Namely: the Bitterroot, Flathead, Kootenai, or the region's major watershed, the Clark Fork. Indeed, all but the Kootenai, which originates in British Columbia and flows through Montana and Idaho before re-entering Canada, are tributary streams to the Clark Fork. All but the very northwestern portion of Montana west of the Continental Divide is drained by the Clark Fork.

We also must climb some steep, broken ridges on either side of the divide and walk for awhile under the broad-limbed ponderosa pine and, further up the mountains, the heavy canopy of Douglas fir and lodgepole pine. For a time, too, we should trod carefully among the ever-present prickly pear and breathe the aromatic sage; climb the rimrocks and marvel at the undulating fields of grain, the starkness of the pattern of strip farming; and, amongst the wilderness, let our spirits soar like the eagles who also call this place home, as we do.

My origins come from two stocks of people: logging, on my father's side, and farming. We grew up in the environment of the woodsworker in northwestern Montana, but the ties remained with my mother's people who farmed and "wheat ranched" in the Highline country near Havre and Dodson. Irish on one side, German on the other. Logger, woodsman, outdoorsman, dirt farmer, lovers of the good, black earth and the rain that sustained them, these people, my family, passed on to me and others of their clan a love for the earth that emanates from it. And, as surely it must have been for our neighbors in their family ties, an unbounding, unabased joy at being in Montana. Consequently, I never suffered the east-west personality split many Montanans do.

It does not matter, east of the Continental Divide or west. Each, distinctly, wraps you in its bosom if you'll let it and clutches your heart unto its unique expression of earthliness, of union, of purpose. I learned this, indelibly, one morning a few years ago when I'd traveled all night from my home west of the Continental Divide to the tiny, windswept town of Dodson in north central Montana. My grandfather had died and we were to bury him this day, in this flat and rolling land that now seemed dreary and uninviting, even sad, compared to the moon-lit mountains I'd left a hundred miles or more behind.

Then, in a burst of time so sudden and so overwhelming it startled me, a flame-red ball, the sun, thrust above the distant horizon. Golden beams of light fanned out across the prairie; the world before me as I drove into the morning was aglow with the

Preceding page:
Kootenai Falls on the Kootenai River between Libby and Troy.

The Absaroka-Beartooth Wilderness. Above: an algae creates the impression of "red" snow.

sun's intensity, its awesome red hugeness. So close, so intimate was its presence that as I faced the first prairie sunrise I can remember "seeing," I understood why my grandfather, the farmer, loved this prairie land so much.

I stopped the car and got out, right along the highway, and let the sun's rays pummel me with their song of joy that called me from my sadness. It was cool yet, the dew still heavy on the nearby fields, but the dazzling warmth of those rays touched me in a way I still, these many years later, do not fully understand. I only knew that, when the sun had finally lifted off the horizon and the day was underway and I resumed my journey on toward Dodson, that I never loved my grandfather more than I did at that moment. I understood now the devotion he'd had for "his" Montana. The good earth, my grandfather's earth, a farmer's earth, aglow in a morning sun, had molded a bond that transcends time and place, and death, and taught me more than I'd been able to understand when he'd told me of them in my boyhood.

Such, it seems, is the emotive relationship of Montana to those who come here, whether to toil or play amidst natures gifts. Many do both, of course.

Agriculture is overwhelmingly Montana's major industry. Approximately half of the state's total income comes from the sale of livestock, crops and livestock products, which is understandable when you realize that more than 62 million of the state's 94 million acres are committed to agriculture.

In the eastern part of the state, i.e., east of the Continental Divide, you might think agriculture was the *only* industry in Montana. Not so even there. Oil and gas, strip mining for coal, tourism and recreation all contribute to the economy even here.

Because of its altitude and low annual precipitation average of fifteen inches, thirteen east and eighteen west of the Continental Divide, Montana is not as productive agriculturally as many other areas in the country. Approximately one-half the land is above 5,000 feet elevation; hence, the growing season in terms of agricultural out-put is somewhat restricted.

Three basic types of agriculture enterprise are used: irrigated farming, grazing and dry farming. Wheat is the predominant crop because it matures more quickly than other grains and its resistance to drought makes it compatible with many Montana soil types. Other basic crops include hay, usually an alfalfa-grass mix, oats, barley, flax, corn, sugar beets, which have declined drastically in recent years, and beans, potatoes and mustard.

Preceding pages:
The Big Hole Valley and Mountains in winter.

In eastern Montana, water is a critically necessary resource. Above photo: the proverbial pot of gold at the end of the rainbow in this case happens to be a haystack.

Some farmers also have experimented recently with sunflowers, but marketing distances present a major disadvantage in terms of competition with farmers in other parts of the country.

Livestock enterprises are mainly beef cattle and sheep, utilizing the major portion of the agricultural acreage in the state. About 2 million acres of Montana land are utilized in irrigated farming, roughly 12 million in dry-land farming operations, and the remaining 48 million in livestock grazing.

Such use exists throughout the state, but drops off notably in terms of percentage west of the Continental Divide. For example, two of the state's western-most counties – Lincoln and Mineral – have only 4.2 and 3.4 percent of their land base, respectively, committed to agriculture. This contrasts with a majority of the counties east of the divide with 90 percent plus of the land committed to agriculture and two, Treasure and Sheridan, listing their land 100 percent committed to agriculture.

Mining takes many forms in Montana. After that first gold flake was discovered in 1852, trains of wagons left for the gold camps. In the years that followed, at least thirty-five different minerals have been produced in commercial quantities in the state.

Copper and petroleum have dominated the industry in recent years. That's changing. Coal is king now, and likely will be for some time. The state is underlain with vast deposits of coal, perhaps as much as 350 *billion* tons, and an energy-hungry world eyes it hungrily. Consequently, stress in the mineral industry in Montana has shifted from the historically-rich Boulder batholith of southwestern Montana, a la Butte and its "Richest Hill on Earth," toward the prairies of north-central and eastern Montana. It's big money that's involved, too. Millions upon millions of dollars are to be made in the big energy push and much of Montana is targeted for future strip mining, oil and gas exploration and the intensive search for uranium. Naturally, there are disagreements, and Montana politics for years to come promises to resound with them.

The coal lies, for the most part, beneath land already intensively used for agriculture. Many ranchers and farmers oppose the mining; some support it, and the debate over its mining, or at the minimum *how* it should be mined, seems interminable.

So does debate over attendant issues. Coal-fired power plants and their umbilical cords to carry electricity to West Coast cities generate much more than kilowatts. The routing of these power transmission lines, their need, and alternative methods of energy transport – including the potential use of existing railroads to ship the coal to the areas

Fall in the Tobacco Root Mountains near Alder.

needing it so they can burn it in their own backyards – are under consideration.

Like agriculture, mining needs, and uses, enormous quantities of water, more, in fact, than is available in arid regions like Montana. Consequently, the debate over resource use and the where and how of converting coal to energy may hinge on the availability of this important resource. Water! You can't live without it in places like Montana, an area that prides itself on the three major watersheds that originate at Triple Divide Peak, the source of water to a continent.

There have been shootings over water in Montana, even in recent years. People are downright possessive of their water rights, be they first, second or what-have-you. So complex is the question of water right ownership that the state undertook a major review of it; research indicates that in some places, like the Bitterroot Valley, water rights have been granted for 300 times as much water as the drainage is capable of producing!

Most of Montana's water is produced west of the Continental Divide. Fifteen percent of the state's land mass produces 58 percent of its water, thanks to the mountainous terrain and the deep snowfall occurring there. The Missouri River and Yellowstone River system drains 82 percent of Montana but yields only 40 percent of its water.

It is west of the divide, too, that another of the state's major industries occurs – timbering. Approximately 20 million acres of Montana is forested, with the major species being coniferous: Douglas fir, ponderosa pine, lodgepole pine, alpine fir, larch, Engelmann spruce, and western white pine.

Much of this land, however, is unavailable for commercial timbering, and properly so. By the mandate of federal law – and 16.7 million acres of those forested lands are in federal ownership – multiple use considerations must prevail in terms of use. Thus, things like soil and watershed protection, wildlife, wilderness, recreation, and aesthetics, legally mandated "multiple uses", preclude cutting in some areas. Generally, however, it is topographic or climatalogical factors that prevent use of national forest land for commercial timbering: steepness of slope, erosion potential, or low productivity in terms of tree growth.

Still, timbering is a major enterprise in the eight counties of western Montana. The timber harvest was 1,171,000,000 board feet in Montana in 1978, but a startling shift in the source of supply has occurred in that decade. In 1969, almost 60 percent of the timber harvested in Montana came from national forest lands. By 1978, that figure had dropped to 38.1 percent.

Clear, cold water flowing from Montana's mountains is a source of delight wherever people, including a young boy, have the opportunity to realize its bounty.

Part of this is due to adjustments by the Forest Service in the face of bitter public concern and congressional hearings. It became apparent in the early 1970s that the national forests were being overcut and that the agency had departed from multiple-use principles. Another is the change in marketable species. As many easy-to-get-to areas of large, old-growth timber were cut out, the industry had to adapt to logging species, like lodgepole pine, that was previously considered noncommercial. The result is that harvesting shifted to areas more immediately accessible and generally that has been on private or state-owned lands. Today, the private lands provide 53.5 percent of the timber harvested in Montana, state lands 2.4 percent, Bureau of Land Management 4.6 percent and Indian reservation land 0.4 percent.

The products of the forest industry are many. Lumber, plywood and veneer, pulp, paper, millwork, Christmas trees, fence posts and railings, particle board, railway ties, utility poles and mining timbers are among their products.

The mountains of western Montana also serve as the focal point of another major Montana industry, tourism and a burgeoning interest in recreational use of the area's unique resources, such as wild rivers, trout fishing, hunting, and backpacking and outfitting trips in the wilderness areas.

Some suggest that the question of natural-land preservation is a new phenomenon in Montana, that the wilderness debate is the result of outside, eastern interests imposing their will on Montana – and other Rocky Mountain states for that matter. That isn't true, and never has been. The preservation mode is part of the Montana tradition. Montana became a state in 1889; preservation of Yellowstone Park, largely at the behest of Montanans, came three short years later and within twenty years a crown gem of the continent would be preserved along the Continental Divide at the north limit of the state.

Glacier National Park is indescribably delicious. In the midst of magnificent mountains, it is a superstar of magnificence. It is breathtaking, particularly along its eastern front where sheer Precambrian sedimentary cliffs storm grandly 7,000 feet above the high prairie and forested valleys.

Its very place names reek with the lore of the Kainah and Piegan Blackfeet who sought their spirit medicine upon its lofty summits. Pitamakin, a woman warrior of the Blackfeet, Two Medicine, Bird Woman Falls, Red Eagle, Little Chief, Piegan Pass, Appitoki Peak, and Almost-a-Dog Mountain are examples.

McDonald Creek, Glacier National Park.

So are Appekuny and Rising Wolf; mountains named for white men who lived with and married into the Blackfeet in the 1800s. Appekuny became one of the finest writers to come out of Montana – James Willard Schultz. It is largely because of him that we have such detailed understanding and insights of the Piegan culture. Much earlier, about 1815, Hugh Monroe, a Hudson's Bay Company trapper had married a Piegan woman. Monroe was probably the first white man in what is now Glacier Park; he became Rising Wolf and he left his name and legends behind.

Glacier needs no legends, however, to stand apart. It exists even today in a distinct niche of the Montana consciousness. Tell most anyone, anywhere in the state, that you've been touring Montana and nine times *out* of ten you'll be asked: "Have you been to Glacier?"

And if you haven't? Well, you haven't really seen Montana. And never mind that

Lower St. Mary Lake.

even in a region where scenic splendor is commonplace, Glacier is idealized as what Montanans *want* others to think the state is. It is the Platonic ideal discovered in reality. Perfection. You can't find mountains more beautiful than these, anywhere. It is the embodiment of inspiration, grandeur, and magnificence; Glacier is mountain country as it should be.

Glacier National Park was established on May 11, 1910, a million-acre preserve with the dual role of providing area where natural processes would dominate and people could seek recreation. The glaciers, some forty of them, that gave the park its name are slowly melting; they'll disappear in time without another ice age. But the mountains, the high cirques, the 200 or more lakes, the waterfalls, and the clear, fast, cold streams will remain.

So, too, will its wildlife – though it's getting more difficult year-by-year to see

Granite Park Chalet with Heaven's Peak in the background.

If Glacier is Montana's inspiration, it doesn't stand alone. Southward from it the Continental Divide has spawned four more areas of special significance. Three are preserved; the fourth isn't and even now, as these words are being written, just into the start of a new century, the drama of people in tension with their dreams is determining the fate of the Rocky Mountain Front.

The Front is an eighty-mile long jut of abrupt limestone reefs where the prairie meets the mountains. It is largely undeveloped public land; to its west, indeed part of it in places are, going south from Glacier, the stunning Great Bear Wilderness, the million-acre Bob Marshall Wilderness, and the Lincoln-Scapegoat Wilderness.

It is, in the words of one of Montana's most revered conservationists, the late Arnold Bolle of Missoula, the "quintessence of wilderness...." Others might agree, but in an almost "never-mind" dismissal of wilderness values, they want to explore beneath it for possible, though improbable, deposits of oil or gas. Caught in the middle is the United States Forest Service, whose mandate under the Wilderness Act is to both preserve the wilderness and accommodate within certain limits those who seek mineral wealth beneath the surface.

The tension that has marked Montana's history will not, it seems, go away. And, as always, that tension involves the relationship of Montanans to their land. The dynamic flows from generation to generation, from one name place to another, but the issues are basically the same, be the battle over grass or plow, cattle or sheep, timber or wilderness, dam or free-flowing river. It is people who compete for the riches, and the limits, of the land; only the times determine what and where.

Victims and benefactors alike of this struggle are the native peoples and other life indigent to a region. In Montana there are, and have been, both – Indians and wildlife. It is apparent neither struggle is over.

Early Montana was home to wandering primitive nomads, hunters. Glacial activity kept them out of the Rockies, but they coursed the high plains immediately east of the mountains. Remnants of their activities, roughly from 10,000 to 4,000 B.C., are occasionally found.

Climatalogical changes about that time brought on a new culture. A semi-arid environment developed on the high plains, wildlife and nomad-hunter alike diminished and gradually disappeared. They eventually were replaced by migrants from the desert Southwest, foragers whose diet used small animals to supplement plants and roots. They

McDonald Falls, Glacier National Park, in winter.

Preceding pages:
Elizabeth Lake, Glacier National Park.

were the Salishan people, whom we know as the Flatheads – anthropologists believe they were the only Indian peoples living in Montana before 1600.

Cultural change, in the form of European man elsewhere on the North American continent, led to the forced migration of other Indian peoples to this part of the world: the Blackfeet, the Atsina or Gros Ventre, Kootenai, Pend Oreille, Crow, Sioux, Cheyenne, Assiniboine, Cree, Chippewa, Metis, but not necessarily in that order.

Of these, the Sioux achieved the most fame, the Blackfeet inspired the most fear. Each earned their reputation.

The Blackfeet, of course, were feared by white and Indian alike. They defended their new-claimed territory from the Continental Divide 300 miles eastward against all comers, no quarter asked. You stayed out of their land or you fought for the privilege of being there, and until most of the 19th Century had lapsed they were left completely alone, the last major "hostile" tribe in the country to be subjugated.

One event catapulted the Sioux people and their leader, Sitting Bull, into the annals of world history – the Battle of the Little Bighorn on June 26, 1876. On that day, they and their Cheyenne allies annihilated the command of Colonel George A. Custer. Custer had badly underestimated the Indians' strength; the result shocked the world and lives today, if still with some reverence, as a tourist attraction. He and his entire command, more than 260 men, left this world on that black day. Not one escaped, surrounded as they were on open hills by a far, far superior force.

Victory had its sting, however. The Custer "massacre" as it was called in non-Indian circles stirred the U.S. government into ending, once and for all, the western Indian problem. A massive military campaign against the "hostiles" ensued. Within a year the Sioux and Cheyenne had been brought to heel. Sitting Bull and his cavalry genius co-leader, Crazy Horse, had won the Battle of the Big Horn but it wasn't enough to win the war.

Nowadays, after more than a century of time, Montana Indian tribes are beginning to reassert themselves. Shunted off, in many cases, to "reservations" representing areas the whites didn't want, the Indians scraped marginal existences out of these lands for two and three generations. Now they flex new-found political muscle; much of their land is under-lain with coal, vast forest reserves invite timbering, and everyone, industry and agriculturalist alike, wants their water.

Preceding page:
On a high point in the Scapegoat Wilderness, looking north, with the Bob Marshall Wilderness ahead as far as the eye can see.

Going-To-Sun Highway
Glacier National Park

Once upon a time the Bureau of Indian Affairs, which administers Indian lands, had jurisdiction over half the land in Montana. Now it's six percent or 5.5 million acres. There are seven Indian reservations in Montana, only one of them west of the Continental Divide. They are:

•*Blackfeet Indian Reservation,* Browning, 1,525,712 acres, northern Montana.

•*Flathead Indian Reservation,* Dixon, 1,242,696 acres, western Montana.

•*Crow Indian Reservation,* Crow Agency, 2,282,764 acres, southeastern Montana.

•*Northern Cheyenne Indian Reservation,* Lame Deer, 444,157 acres, southeastern Montana.

•*Fort Peck Indian Reservation,* Wolf Point, 2,093,124 acres, northeastern Montana.

•*Fort Belknap Indian Reservation,* Fort Belknap Agency, 651,119 acres, southeastern Montana.

•*Rocky Boy Indian Reservation,* Rocky Boy, 107,613 acres, northeastern Montana.

Of this total of 8,343,929 acres, 33 percent of land within the reservation boundaries is owned by non-Indians.

If talk of the Custer debacle and the Blackfeet raid still linger in the Montana memory, they're eclipsed by an even greater romance, the cowboy and the man who immortalized him, Charles Marion Russell.

Russell pervades the Montana psyche. His artistry of the Old West sustains an imagery, a time, a legend Montanans don't want to let go. Painter, sculptor, story-teller, Charles Russell embodied in his art the essence of Montana in transition from frontier to pioneer times. He did it with a brush so powerful, colors so rich and accurate that historians and layman alike would use his canvasses to glimpse the bygone days he romanticized.

He came to Montana in 1880 from St. Louis, a sixteen-year-old cowhand whose keen observation and artistic hands would ultimately lead to international fame. The years have served only to deify him: "Charlie" Russell prints can be found hanging on the walls of restaurants, homes, doctor's offices, and bars everywhere in Montana. He is indelible upon his adopted land.

Two historic edifices bear his name: the Charles M. Russell Gallery in Great Falls and the Montana State Historical Society Museum in Helena. Each is worth visiting. So

The late John Clarke of East Glacier, shown here in 1968, became internationally renowned as a young man for his woodcarvings, including one of a mountain goat that was termed "anatomically perfect" when presented to the Museum of Plains Indians. Clarke had created the carving fully thirty years previous.

do countless schools and one of the most magnificent stretches of the awesome wilderness he painted so vividly, the sprawling Charles M. Russell National Wildlife Refuge along the Missouri River in north-central Montana.

I grew up in a home where Russell's active, participant historical mood prevailed. A rich and powerful print of his painting *"When Tracks Spell Meat"* always hung, at my father's insistence, in my parents' home. It shows an elk hunter astride a horse, naturally, in Montana's snow-covered high country just after he's downed a six-point bull elk. It was a good, big print with full, rich rendition of Russell's mute colors, powerful in the purple hues he handled so well. I always knew it hung in our home because it captured the unique dimension of Montana, the mountains and the challenge of elk hunting, that best expressed my father's kinship to the Montana mountains. Did it also, I've often wondered, help shape and define that kinship?

Other painters have followed in Russell's footsteps; all have felt the frustration of his contemporaries, Olaf Seltzer and Edgar Paxson and Winold Reiss. If you paint in Montana, you will work in the shadow of Charles Marion Russell.

Still, a renaissance of realistic western and wildlife art is underway in Montana today. Its center is the picturesque Flathead Valley; indeed a literal colony of artists sprung up there and in nearby regions the closing decades of the just-concluded century.

Among the best: artists like the late sculptor Bob Scriver of Browning, whose immense works commanded $100,000 or more; Gary Schildt of Kalispell, a gifted and sensitive painter and sculptor; Ace Powell, who was personally encouraged to paint by Russell; and wildlife artist Elmer Sprunger of Bigfork, who lives and works on the shores of picturesque Flathead Lake. Robert F. Morgan of Helena, renowned for his historical presentations on canvas, particularly of the Lewis & Clark Expedition, is another. All are Montana natives, and all portray aspects of the Montana scene that are at once historical and timeless.

Scriver, who worked with intensity and grand vision, acquired an international reputation with sculptures so powerfully conceived and executed that the bronze seems to throb with the story of life they portray. So it is, too, with the meticulous realism Sprunger brushes into his canvases of Montana wildlife, ranging from exquisite renderings of mountain birds as well as the majestic elk. Like Scriver and the part-Blackfoot Schildt, Sprunger sees his role as prophetic, and like so much of what you find in Montana, it concerns a land and its people. "Wildlife tell you what's happening to the land as one species gives way to another. They are the forerunners. They're out in the world affected by everything we do, while we kind of think we can stay in the background," Sprunger said.

Wildlife, incidentally, still plays an important role in Montana. Hunting and fishing are major recreational endeavors. Trapping is a sizeable enterprise. But so are nonconsumptive uses of wildlife. Interest has grown in recent years in the so-called

The late Ace Powell in his studio in Kalispell.

nongame species and the various refuges and preserves have become popular attractions year around, as has the proliferation of "viewable wildlife" programs.

Among the more celebrated are the National Bison Range at Moiese, in the lower Flathead Valley in western Montana, where the American buffalo was saved from extinction, Glacier and Yellowstone National Parks, and that most astounding of all wildlife refuges in the state, the previously mentioned Charles M. Russell National Wildlife refuge in north-central Montana.

The CMR, as it's known locally, sprawls along the breaks of the Missouri River for 125 miles and it's doubtful if any other single place on the North American continent plays host to the variety of wildlife inhabiting this one refuge.

Elk are found there and so are mule deer and antelope. There are badgers and coyotes, prairie dogs by the thousands, perhaps an endangered blackfooted ferret or two, bighorn sheep, porcupine, red foxes, spotted skunks, whitetailed jackrabbits, spotted

Artist Elmer Sprunger in his studio in Bigfork.

This rich painting by artist Robert F. Morgan of Helena shows Captain William Clark, Joseph Fields, John Potts and York of the Lewis and Clark Expedition overlooking the Helena Valley with Prickly Pear Creek at the bottom. The 44½ x 35¼ oil on canvas painting is titled "Captain Clark Overlooking Helena Valley, July 19, 1805," and is one of many historical paintings done by Morgan, who also is curator-emeritus of the Montana Historical Society.

hares, raccoon, beaver, mink, muskrat, the kit fox, the rattlesnake, king snake, and numerous rodents.

Forty-five mammal species are known to live on the refuge, but that's small pickings compared to bird life. Over 210 separate species have been recorded on the refuge's million acres, of which approximately 80 percent are year-long residents. And that isn't all! The Missouri River contains life, too. Northern pike, sauger, walleye, paddlefish, sturgeon, rainbow and brown trout, and several other fish species swim its waters.

Among the bird species, we find an incredible variety. Eagles, hawks, geese, ducks, osprey, the prairie falcon, sharp-tailed grouse, grey partridge, Merriam's turkey, doves, and pheasants fly there. So do the great horned owl, burrowing owl, short-eared owl, and others. And sandhill cranes, long-billed curlew, the American widgeon, shoveler, killdeer, common snipe, American avocet, mourning dove, variety of thrushes, woodpeckers, swallows, crows, warblers, sparrows, shrikes and wrens.

No picture of Montana is complete without considering its wildlife. More than ninety species of mammals are identified within it, with the spring-legged mule deer probably the most wide-spread of the larger species. So are elk and whitetail deer, grizzly and black bears, coyote, the fox, a few of the endangered timber wolves, and numerous more.

Furbearers like the beaver, mink, lynx, pine marten and others support a major trapping industry. And there are hundreds of birds, including one of the rarest species in the world – the trumpeter swan, which makes its home in the Red Rock Lakes region of extreme southern Montana.

Most wildlife species are spread out across the land, but some concentrate in areas specifically preserved for them. The trumpeter is an example; it was literally brought back from near-extinction just sixty-some years ago to a sizeable population at the Red Rock Lakes National Wildlife Refuge in the Centennial Valley.

The two national parks are, of course, wildlife preserves; both being of significant value to the survival of certain species, like the buffalo in Yellowstone and the grizzly bear in both Glacier and Yellowstone. Numerous national wildlife refuges dot the state,

The Missouri River is central to the breaks country of the C.M. Russell National Wildlife Refuge. This cherished area has now been given national monument status.

most serving as vital links in the life system of migratory waterfowl, though all have year-around resident populations of several wildlife species.

Portions of these refuges are open to visitors, though seasonal limitations at critical times – like the nesting season – rule out intrusions of any kind. The largest of these refuges is, of course, the Charles M. Russell, which has a rather comprehensive road system open to visitors. Smaller refuges include the Lee Metcalf Refuge in the Bitterroot Valley, Pishkun, Willow Creek and Benton Lake refuges in the Augusta-Choteau-Great Falls area immediately east of the Continental Divide, Lake Bowdoin near Malta, and the Medicine Lake Refuge in the extreme northeastern part of the state. And, just recently an exceptionally beautiful new and needed refuge in northwestern Montana, the Lost Trail National Wildlife Refuge near Marion was added to this legacy.

Hunting and fishing are major seasonal activities in Montana. Both attract international attention. Areas like the Bob Marshall Wilderness and the sprawling Beaverhead National Forest in southwestern Montana are famous elk-hunting haunts. Added to that are several major streams, with two frontrunners, the Madison and Yellowstone Rivers, considered to be among the world's best trout-fishing waters.

A sizeable outfitting industry has built up around both passions. Summer and fall horseback trips carry "dudes" and serious outdoorsmen alike into the remote wilderness for whatever purpose, be it fishing, hunting, sightseeing, photography, or simple nature appreciation.

A growing passion is river floating, particularly in the western part of the state where challenging whitewater attracts serious kayakers and rafters. But fishing remains the major endeavor on the thousands of Montana streams and lakes.

Small wonder, too. Montana boasts 450 miles of "blue ribbon" trout streams-the best there is, anywhere. Streams like the Madison, upper Yellowstone, Big Horn, Gallatin, Big Hole, and portions of the Missouri harbor brown and rainbow trout in greater numbers and size than you can imagine.

Fishing pressure has increased in recent years, however, and contemplative fishing values are being emphasized now. Catch-and-release is promoted. Smaller keep limits are being imposed each year, and in some areas – particularly on the popular Madison – severe restrictions have been implemented to provide stretches where no float-fishing takes place.

One solution has been to spread fishing pressure out. Other Montana streams offer fishing of quality equal to its more well-known waters. Over 1,000 miles of the state's streams are labeled "red ribbon" streams. In most parts of the country they'd be considered fantastic trout fisheries. So would the 2,437 miles of "yellow ribbon" streams, and many of the lesser tributaries in the mountain country that are incredible producers of the area's native cutthroat trout.

A majority of Montanans fish. They consider it part of their way of life; more and more, with the advent of technological devices like safe "rubber" rafts and ripstop nylon backpacking equipment and snowmobiles, Montanans work and pursue recreation year-around.

What's it like to live in Montana? What sort of people actually *live* there. For one thing, you're constantly aware of the climate – and the saying is that if you're not, wait a few minutes. It's bound to change.

Most people outside Montana think of it, naively perhaps, as a land always locked in snow and tormented by blizzards and whatever other terrible things happen on the high plains or in the mountains. Untrue as that naive and uninformed picture is, some Montanans would like to promote it. That reputation has helped keep the state's population on the low side, still under a million in a nation whose official 2000 census was 281,421,906.

In that 2000 census, Montana's population was 902,195. This figured out to a density of 6.2 persons to the square mile, as compared to the national average of 57.5. That statistic is misleading, however. In vast portions of Montana the figure is zero people per square mile. Population is concentrated in low-land area, key cities and popular recreation areas, as anybody in the Bitterroot, Flathead or Gallatin valleys could tell you.

Montana is a rural, agrarian society. But it's also urban, as redistricting under the one-man, one-vote mandate proved. Political power in Montana shifted to the urban areas in keeping with population shifts that have altered the state's political structure. Some realized this change with sadness. The era of the state's historical "cowboy legislature" was over. The one-cow, one vote era had given way to that of the one man-

Preceding pages:
Western larch after a heavy frost in the fall near the small town of Trego in
northwestern Montana, where the author lived as a boy.

—84—

one vote.

Seven counties now account for more than half the Montana population. They include counties with major cities: Yellowstone (Billings), Cascade (Great Falls), Missoula (Missoula), Silver Bow (Butte), Flathead (Kalispell), Lewis and Clark (Helena) and Gallatin (Bozeman). Of these, three contain fully a third of Montana's residents. They are Yellowstone and Cascade east of the Continental Divide and Missoula to the west.

As in most things concerning Montana, however, you can't generalize. As urban as some areas might be, about one-half the state's population resides in towns under 1,000 population, thus they reflect, socially and politically, a definite rural orientation. The state's smallest "official" communites, of 135 officially so listed, are Cardwell in Jefferson County at 40 and Antelope at 43 in Sheridan County. The largest? Well Billings outstrips any other community at 89,847.

Trends seem to indicate that the urbanization process will continue. Major changes began to occur in the mid-and late 1970s, and they've continued to this day, as rampant subdivision activity took place in the Flathead, Gallatin, Missoula, Great Falls, Helena and Billings area – as well as the picturesque Bitterroot Valley that Father Point called the place better than anywhere else. This valley, blessed with a milder winter climate than most of Montana, serves as a "bedroom community" for industries and businesses located in nearby Missoula. Its people growth over the past two decades has been overwhelming.

What are the expectations? An excellent publication called *"Montana in Maps"* put it well: "With the exception of Butte and Anaconda, (where mining and smelting activities declined) Montana cities have experienced rapid growth, small towns have remained stable or shown slow growth, and farm population has steadily declined as farm sizes increase."

Consequently, Montana marches into the opening years of this century as it did the last two: its people and their way of life being shaped by the land itself, by its resources, and by the hopes and dreams they bring to bear against or for it.

Montana is still a state of mind. And more!

Preceding page:
Fall colors, Charles M. Russell National Wildlife Refuge.
Opposite page:
Beargrass, Glacier National Park.

The Bitterroot, Montana's state flower.

Opposite page:
Fog enshrouds the valley
below Stryker Mountain
in northwestern Montana.

Rock slide in the Sapphire mountains. Above: marmot in the rocks.

Montana sunset, Bitterroot Mountains.

Floaters "on the bubble" as their raft enters the rapids at Spruce Park on the wild Middle Fork of the Flathead River, Great Bear Wilderness. Above: a young fishermen displays his first big brown trout taken on a salmon fly imitation, Big Hole River.

Preceding pages:
Evening on the trail near the confluence of Granite Creek and the Middle
Fork of the Flathead River, Great Bear Wilderness.

Opposite page:
Canyon on the Boulder River.

Ghost buildings along the Missouri River.

A mule deer doe checks things out along the North Fork of the Flathead River.

Reflections on a snow-melt pond in alpine country. Above: emergence!

Last touch of sunlight in late evening, Glacier National Park. Above: on full alert!

The changing face of the Lower Falls of the Yellowstone River, Yellowstone National Park. Above: Old Faithful.

Opposite page:
Mountains on both sides of the view,
Selway-Bitterroot Wilderness.

A web in the wilderness, Bunker Creek drainage, South Fork of the Flathead River. Above: Pretty as a picture in Glacier National Park.

Preceding pages:
Absaroka-Beartooth Wilderness.

Opposite page:
At the headwaters of the Missouri River.

Sentinel of a by-gone era, southwestern Montana.

Preceding pages:
Lone fisherman on the Middle Fork of the Flathead River,
Great Bear Wilderness.

Opposite page:
On a high ridge overlooking the
upper Whitefish Range in northwestern Montana.

Tightening the cinch.

Opposite page:
Artist's observation perch on the
shore of Flathead Lake.

Norris Geyser Basin, Yellowstone National Park. Above: Abandoned cabin.

CLOSED

AREA BEHIND THIS SIGN IS
CLOSED TO HUMAN TRAVEL
DANGEROUS BEAR

*Sharing an afternoon along the Madison River in Yellowstone National
Park. Above: another aspect of the outdoor experience in Yellowstone*

Opposite page:
Fall colors in the
upper Whitefish Range.

Along the trail in the Selway-Bitterroot Wilderness. Above: Packing the string, Bob Marshall Wilderness.

Hunting camp at sunset in the Bob Marshall Wilderness. Above: bighorn rams.

Preceding pages:
Evening sun sculpts a line of cliffs on the Beaverhead National Forest.

Opposite page:
Cascade on Kootenai Creek, Selway-Bitterroot Wilderness.

Varying shades of fall, Ruby River drainage.

Preceding pages:
Tracks in the snow on a cold day, Gravelly Range.

Opposite page:
On the trail into the wilderness, Lolo National Forest.

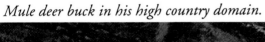
Mule deer buck in his high country domain.

Porcupine digging for food at the onset of winter. Above: a pair of porcupines about as high as they can go.

Opposite page:
Headwaters freshet.

Mission Mountains. Above: Mid-stream encounter, Middle Fork of the Flathead River.

Island of mountains in the prairie. Above: A pair to draw to.

The broad, deep waters of the main Flathead River downstream from Flathead Lake. Above: On full alert.

Preceding pages:
Island of color.

Opposite page:
Bounty from the high country.

Inviting forest road, early fall.

Preceding pages:
Snowcrest Range in southwestern Montana on a day the sun was kept from
warming the earth.

Opposite page:
Clinging to life in the shadows of a cliff.

Coulee in Prairie County north of Terry in eastern Montana.

Opposite page:
Lupine, Helena National Forest.

Ahern Lake, Glacier National Park. Above: Lodgepole pine
in the high country.

Dry fly in quest of cutthroat trout on the Middle Fork of the Flathead River.
Above: Streambank detail.

Elk at Gibbon Meadows, Yellowstone National Park. Above: dropping into field of beargrass in bloom, Bunker Creek, Flathead National Forest.